Meraki

Meraki
Written by Harshita Ray, Alisha Rai, Adwita Agrahari, Divita Joshi
and Shreya Banerji
Print Edition

First Published in India in 2021
Inkfeathers Publishing
New Delhi 110095

Content and Cover Design Copyright © Harshita Ray, Alisha Rai,
Adwita Agrahari, Divita Joshi and Shreya Banerji, 2021

All rights reserved.

ISBN 978-93-90882-32-8

Without limiting the rights under copyright reserved above, no part of this publication may be reproduced, lent, resold, or transmitted by any means, electronic, mechanical, photocopying or otherwise, without the prior permission of both the copyright owner and the publisher of this book.

www.inkfeathers.com

Meraki

Harshita Ray, Alisha Rai, Adwita Agrahari

Divita Joshi and Shreya Banerji

Inkfeathers Publishing

to my future self, make sure you look back here
-Harshita

to my Kindergarten teacher, Mrs. Rusveen Singh
-Alisha

to those, who both find and lose themselves in books
-Adwita

to Kanchi, Luka, Huskie, and Bootle
-Divita

to forgotten poets, unrecognised artists, Arlo and my muse-them.
-Shreya

Contents

Preface   xi

1. One-Way Light   1
2. Two Roads   2
3. Asterism   3
4. Youth   4
5. The Art of Destruction   6
6. Rip Current   7
7. Artificial   8
8. Running on Air   9
9. 5-4-3-2-1   10
10. If You Belong to a Broken Home   11
11. Catch-22   12
12. Antagonist   13
13. Dreaming, Running   14
14. Deluge   15
15. My Pain was My Addiction   16
16. August   17
17. The Ladder to The Roof   19
18. Deliquesce   21

19.	The Wolf, the Snake, the Crow & I	22
20.	Late Night Nostalgia	24
21.	Ruminating	25
22.	The Ripple Effect	26
23.	Selcouth	27
24.	$F = qE + qv \times B$	28
25.	Trust Issues	29
26.	Loathe Myself	30
27.	Endless Art Galleries	31
28.	Epinephrine	32
29.	Naka-Choko	33
30.	Hell	34
31.	Wolves	35
32.	Rhythm and Blues	36
33.	Avarice	37
34.	Scenery	38
35.	To Be a Poet	39
36.	Red Ink Street	40
37.	Fuel	41
38.	Who We Were, Who We Are	42
39.	Haemorrhage	44
40.	The Fragments of a Memory	45
41.	Calling Constellation	46
42.	Twin Flames	48
43.	Connotation	49

44.	Fortissimo	50
45.	Mortality	51
46.	Valiant	52
47.	Reverie	53
48.	Mithridatism	54
49.	Girdling	56
50.	Outlook	57
51.	Combat, Punch	58
52.	Deception	59
53.	Recherché	60
54.	Default Network Mode	61
55.	Yearning	62
56.	Silly Girl	63
57.	Monochromatic	65
58.	Azoth	66
59.	End Line	68
60.	To My Friend	70
	Acknowledgements	71
	Meet the Co-Authors	75

Preface

Meraki

(v.) to do something with soul, creativity or love; to put something of yourself into your work.

And that's exactly what five teenagers did, sitting miles away from each other. The decision of writing Meraki became the highlight of an otherwise ordinary December morning of 2020. Soon, ideas poured over, about everything from the book title to the theme. The thought of leaving this project unfinished haunted us, but we persevered, and here we are!

Of course, writing Meraki was no ordinary scenario of angsty, hormonal teenagers writing away about their high school sweethearts. No, there was camaraderie, love, laughter and just enough arguments to make the friendship healthy. It's been a hundred something days, we don't really keep count, but a couple of hundred days spent for a lifetime of immortalisation.

The question still stands: Why did we do this?

For the good-old sake of storytelling! These five burnt out but passionate teenagers want to tell their stories. Moreover, we want you to know that you are not alone in how you feel.

We were heavily inspired by self-expression, all the pieces you will read further took time, emotion and hard work. Needless to say, it is straight from our hearts and minds. Art saved us, so if you have something to say or write: it will save you too.

We hope you relish our work every time you open this chest of treasured memories.

Best wishes,

Harshita, Alisha, Adwita, Divita and Shreya

Meraki

One-Way Light

Living and yearning. Yearning for when it will all be perfect, a utopian state of life. A stretch of never-ending ticking clocks, it is nowhere and it is everywhere, it is a one-way light, once lost, doesn't come back, with the power that it holds, how dare we try to put it in a word, 'time'.

The wait has no duration, for it is intense. The wait is love, the wait is pain, the wait is ache. You didn't ache for me. Yet, here I was, my eyes blinded. My days were years, my nights, centuries! I lost age, lost any form. My soul sat dismal, buoyant on the guilt of having destroyed it all.

Killing time, I kill time. No, time is killing me.

Two Roads

I find it ironic how we know so little about ourselves. But there is a strange comfort in uncertainty, to not know who you'll meet and which moments can change your life and you have to take that journey. To walk between the two roads of *who you are and who you can be.*

Asterism

I stand on the edge of the cliff,
looking down at the water,
under the inky sky
chatoyant with stars and constellations unremembered.
The still water gently tugs at the land,
and with it, the tiny, glistening specks of the sky move.
I let the ground slip under my feet as I fall into the sea of stars.
You don't have to fly to reach the stars.

Youth

Shopping sprees and McDonald's drive-through, hair whipping in the cold, hard wind as the two-wheeler drives past in the copper-yellow glow of streetlights. One night, a movie is on the menu; the next, a quick trek in the nearby hills.

Visiting cafes, drinking coffee, reading in the sunlight. Eating together, in the abandoned parks; the creaking of the rickety swings while passing around some cola and munching on candy, the smell of rust and dust, centres of palms coated with a dull red.

Summer greets us with swimsuits and sweltering heat, we embrace it with air conditioners and shaved ice. Belting songs off-key with all the wrong words, laughing hysterically at every clumsy dance step, because who is anyone to stop us?

Suddenly, our breaths leave trails of fog and each syllable we utter has a shadow of its own. Rubbing our hands together, touching the cold tip of our red nose. The heat seeps out and a bitter cold pleasantly settles over us.

Walks in the darkest hour of the night, lazily talking into the early hours of the morning, as the sun shows its first colours at dusk.

The sun rises differently for us; tiptoeing around the horizon, waiting patiently for conversation to die out, appearing as we fall asleep under the cool morning air.

The Art of Destruction

I wish to witness the day when
The Sun's heat sets the forests ablaze,
The ocean waters engulf the land,
The wind unleashes her wrath
And the land cracks open.
"Destruction is an art in itself."
It isn't the end, but the provenance of something new.

(To be read when the world ceases to exist.)

Rip Current

It's a sinking feeling. Like drowning in multiple oceans, and with every second, you are only submerging. To know it was never meant to be, even after it happened. We ask, if it happened, why on Earth can't it be? We are born with the answer—of course, everything's made to break—we live, but with the knowledge of death. Why, oh, why, is it laborious then, to accept loss, the breaking of our hearts?

Artificial

What is wrong with this generation? A whole generation of fools who believe beauty is pain and romanticize insanity. Chasing after perfect bodies and perfect faces. Flawless skin isn't what you need to strive for and hiding every scar behind layers of makeup shouldn't be your motive. Start living in your truth.

Running on Air

I reminisce about a time when I used to hope without any qualms. It was so easy, having hope, huddled into a little corner of anticipation and confidence. I wasn't afraid to fall because the slight glint of hope kept me going, the possibility of failure seemed absurd.

It was like flying, the uncertainty of it all sent waves of dizziness coursing through and a vision of the future flashed before my eyes. It was easy to dream, and it felt like running on air.

But now, it's not as easy to hand out hope. Reality tore the wings of assurance and sent me tumbling to the never-ending abyss of disappointment. I fell too many times, crashed too hard and lost the naivete of the person I once was. I miss the feeling of flying, the inevitability and freedom.

Now I go through life with my feet on the ground and head in the clouds of self-doubt. Hope seems like a distant thing, non-existent even. I refuse to let hope spark, knowing all too well how much misery it brings. How can something that's supposed to be a beacon for happiness be so harrowing? It's an aphorism, constantly chanting in my brain and getting louder each time. Something that I once found thrilling, now only contributes to a longing, for something so simple yet daring.

Running on air never felt more impossible.

5-4-3-2-1

The light at the end of a dark cavern is non-existent.

The truth is, it isn't a dank cavern we often find ourselves thrown into. It's a thick, wooden box that shrinks every second, making it laborious to breathe, strenuous to move, impossible to live.

At some point, I drink my own spit and feel it travel down my dry throat, excruciatingly slowly. My limbs are sore, body aches from trying to fit comfortably in. Splinters pierce my palms, but the pounding in my head distracts me from every tiny speck of wood entering my body.

The anxiety attack, I graciously bestow upon myself, makes the box feel like metal and impenetrable. I wait for the light, but it never comes. It's surprising I ever believed in its existence.

If You Belong to a Broken Home

You're the child with a broken childhood,
Seeking validation with utter desperation from parents whose attention you shouldn't have to beg for.

You have been used to hearing the raised voice of your father, the silent sobbing of your mother. You know this to be the reality of the world. "Husband and wife often fight, it only shows their love."

To you, abuse is love;
Degradation is love;

And so, when they do the bare minimum, it is astonishing. It's new. It doesn't feel like home. If this is your story, I am so sorry and I assure you- you are not alone.

Catch-22

It's a dilemma. You were lost, your eyes all dreamy, beautiful and dreamy, but I hated them, they didn't look at me the same way they did she, they didn't glisten, bother, they would stay affixed on her, ever so delicate self, soft skin, sweet talking. I? Oh, a mere simpleton. Hands rough, mouth boisterous, hair short and wild. I wasn't her, never could be. How could you have ever loved me? The dilemma, you ask? Do I stay or do I leave?

Antagonist

He saw himself as the bad guy in our story, the villain perhaps. And that's exactly what he forced himself to become, he forced himself to destroy anything and everything that was left of us. He couldn't blame anyone else for holding him at gunpoint except himself, manifesting all his animosity and remorse from pure emotions into a meteorite.

Dreaming, running

I see her in front of me, morose and eyes brimming with tears. I stare in horror as she looks right at me, mimicking my every move. Unspoken words ring loud in the hollow of my skull.

(*you're not good enough,* comes her thin voice)

I turn around and run but the voices don't stop. I can't see her but she keeps deriding me, in words spoken with feigned compassion.

(*look at the others,* she says, softly)

In those moments filled with gentle whispers of virulence that caress my skin, the world seems dizzying. I keep running as the ground below vanishes, the silent screams of asking her to stop- lost in the peace of freedom.

(*do better.*)

I don't stop running.
dreaming, running, dreaming, running.

I wake up in cold sweat and dread fills my insides, as I see her right in front of me,
again.

Deluge

That night as the storm was churning in the pit of my stomach, I braced myself for the pain I would have to endure. Someone once said: ridding yourself of pain is running towards it. I wondered, lying in cold sweats on my sheets if it was true. If tonight would be one where the trembling of my bones and shuddering of my heart would cease.

If the sun would show its rusty rays and illuminate parts of myself, I consider flawed. And when this new light has been shed on the evidence of the body I have chosen to neglect, the war inside will make peace with itself.

My Pain was My Addiction

And when I tried to break free from the shackles which bounded me, I felt my soul bleed.

I was so familiar with the idea of being chained, glorifying the pain it caused me

so much so that even escape felt foreign.

My pain was my addiction.

August

August
Was when we remembered time.

Today, I learnt
The stars are just a blanket over the land;
A world exists beyond
Our little grass meadows and
Feeble, bamboo houses,
Yet you and I run
Our rugged palms through
The dew on the damp August leaves.

A world exists beyond
Father's rude words and
Stable chores,

Your mother is unaware, long asleep
Under the twilight
When I sit under the moon

Asking her questions, she is forbidden to answer.

Will I see your silhouette tonight
Peeping from behind the well

Will I see you
This August night?

The Ladder to The Roof

"Look at me
And don't look down"
Ten feet above the ground and
The fear of falling
Was drowning me.

"Look at me!"
So, I looked at him.
Stared straight into his eyes
And suddenly
It wasn't the fear of falling
Off the ladder
That terrified me.

He stretched out his hand so I took it and clambered onto the roof.

And so,
Two kids spent the rest of their day
Talking about

Alisha | 20

The sky and the trees
And the birds and their dreams.

As if nothing
Could ever go wrong.

Deliquesce

The grass blades whisper against my skin,
the leaves sigh in contentment,
and,
As the blood flows through my fingers and seeps into the ground,
tiny seedlings sprout from the earth,
breaking through the confines.
If you listen closely, you can hear the gentle splinter of the dried mud as the sapling emerges,
and with it,
I slowly abate into the dust.
As I silently bleed into the earth,
the air around feels pungent and heavy,
though the flutter of wings,
the stillness of water and
the song of the wind,
pacify my senses, as I close my eyes one last time.

The Wolf, the Snake, the Crow & I

And when I stepped into the forest land,
My shoulder was tapped roughly by a hand.
There, on its hind feet a wolf stood,
Rubbing its paws, cunningly, as a wolf should.

"Come my way, miss, come my way;
The place I know is the place to stay;
'Tis a small house with flowers plenty;
Brick-walled, bare and empty!"

Apprehensively, I took a step forward,
Toward the wolf, heading sunward
When my feet were tied suddenly,
Said a coaxing snake insistently:

"The mistake of following him is grave,
Listen to me, come to my cave;
We shall lavishly dine,
Then rest under the soft moonshine!"

Enticing was the offer it was making,
So, I traced the path it was taking,
But before I could even move
I heard the bass of a groove

"Stop right there, if you wish to be saved,
Corrupt & selfish, this snake plans to enslave the depraved;

Accompany me; the thump of my tune
Will guide you out this site of gloom!"
Croaked the voice of a crow,
Up above, from the branches of melted snow;

I saw myself surrounded
By choices that left me confounded;

One of three roads, I was asked to take,
Instead, I split into three so I could partake,
In enjoying the gifts of all;
My spirit will tell you: I had a ball!

To the vibrant flowers, my hands tended,
While my mouth wolfed down the feast I attended;
The leaves crunched beneath my feet as I danced;
At the blood on the ground, nobody glanced.

Late Night Nostalgia

There are nights when I wonder if you've been well.

Do you still play your guitar or question the existence of everything when you lose yourself to your thoughts, tossing like the waves of the sea?

Do you still ponder upon our conversations, both meaningless and meaningful?

I wonder if you're still the same.

There are days when I wonder what we could have been,

probably destroy and be destroyed with the proximity of one another but the inkling sure is tempting,

I care still maybe I always will.

Ruminating

Nostalgia, perhaps one's greatest weakness but also the most mystical emotion. How so effortlessly, do I wander in my own head and pick one memory—perhaps dust it off the shelves because I haven't visited it in a long time, and just watch. Watch myself laughing with friends, watch myself fall in love. I just listened to the song I loved three years ago and I was 14 once again. I can almost smell the pizza from my best friends' twelfth birthday. I can hear our faint laughter, our shoes clicking against the ground while we ran into the night, when our only fear was being discovered by the seeker. I can see the crowd cheering at those matches that I played, I am able to feel the happiness from when we were still friends. I want to go back, but I can't. Perhaps, that is the power of time, of nostalgia. That we can never take advantage of it.

The Ripple Effect

It starts as a small drop, insignificant. Maybe it was a simple smile or a 'hello'. One smile leads to another and that one drop adds to an ocean of benevolence. You say you want to be remembered long after you're gone and your kindness did exactly that. One smile, one compliment, one greeting, led to someone else's smile which led to another's, and that one gesture melted a frozen ocean altogether.

Selcouth

I feel like the centre of the universe.

Worries seem to dissipate into the earth and tranquillity settles in the small shades of blue in the sky as the clouds languidly travel above. Rows of primroses hide from the vivid sun rays behind the gentle slope of the hill.

I let the breeze caress my skin and feel comforted, at home. It feels familiar, even if completely foreign. Butterflies settle over the flowers, their vibrant colours soothing my nerves. A fluttering butterfly perches itself on the back of my palm. I feel my heart racing with exhilaration.

The dew on the petals of the primroses glistens as the sunlight kisses them, bathing them in its warmth. My feet sink into the mud, soft and moist. *I could stay here forever*, I think. Momentarily, the butterfly disintegrates, grey and paper-thin wings fall to the ground. *Could I?*

$$F = qE + qv \times B$$

There is a motor underneath my bed. I do not know how it works. My brothers do. Something about gears and batteries and electromagnets.

Doesn't strike my fancy, really. It should. I am told it should.

My deep sleep keeps me ignorant to the slow rotation of my bed. How can I stop a good night's sleep? This fluffy mattress lures me in and in minutes, not the loudest of sounds can disturb my slumber.

My indifference to change is taken for granted. The motor takes a one- eighty degrees turn. I know there is a motor under me. It growls and bellows.

Every day, I wake up on the wrong side of the bed. Maybe I should sleep less often. Catch the motor in action. Research about it for a change.

Remove the batteries. Spite it by placing them back in wrong.

This isn't an interesting story. It is me being shirty and peckish. crying about switching off a motor. Surely, it isn't a tough task. Is it? I would not know. I know nothing about nothing.

Trust Issues

'Trust Issues' is just a more basic, seemingly less pessimistic term for cynicism. Deep down, we all know that humans cannot be trusted. They will tear each other apart, reduce each other to fragments of disenchantment and incredulity at the first prospect they get. Isn't that the reformed and more appropriate definition of humanity now?

We know because we are the monsters our parents had warned us about. We are humans.

Loathe Myself

You look in the mirror and wrinkle your face in disgust. Skimming your belly and thighs, 'too fat, too thick!' you cry. Didn't she look so good in her new post?

You slow dance into the song of superficial social media. It is a trance, but how must you know? Too dark, too skinny, too fat, too ugly!

You exclaim. I hate myself!

On the other end of the screen, the model screams the same in her lonesome bedroom.

Today, I am angry. Angry at the pit in my stomach, at the empty but pensive cavity in my chest. Today, my demons have escaped my head. They are creating pandemonium in my body but I am much too numb to feel it. Help me feel! I yell at my demons. They only scoff at my misery. They don't want to make me feel. Why are they not coming back? They are tired of inhabiting this lifeless body. Today, I wreak the foul stench of my unsatisfied soul.

Endless Art Galleries

I've always admired art.
Art, in any form.
Maybe that was because
It was the way other people
Could express my emotions for me.

And then we grew up.
Focused more on our brushstrokes
Instead of our muse.
The paintbrush was in my hand,
But I wasn't the one painting.

Free yourself
From the shackles of ordinary life.
Run where the wind takes you,
Emancipate yourself.

For only the blind
critique the artists' work
for art is everything
But simple.

Epinephrine

The fight or flight response. An involuntary human reaction to situations of danger or threat to survival. The figure comes closer and my body shudders with fear.

I see a hint of light at the end of the tunnel. I rush towards it, looking for any kind of escape as it nears. I run on the seemingly never-ending asphalt, clutching my wound weakly. I can feel the adrenaline surging and pulsing in my body. My mind begs me to flee so I run faster to the end of this crevasse. Because running away is easy; standing your ground is hard.

I reach for the ray of light and my hand goes right through it. I feel dread slowly taking over as it nears and the walls start to close in. I realise there's no escape and there's only one thing I can do. Fight.

I turn around and clench my shaky fists.

Naka-Choko

The bite of my food
Should taste like
Stretch marks,
Disgusted reflections and
Daily weigh-ins
With sharp inhales.
Instead
Sweet and sour sing
In symphony on my tongue.

Hell

I love the way I tremble when your darkness sweeps me off my feet

the sweet scent of destruction we know all too well

you make me relive the guilt for crimes you commit- like my own personal hell

Wolves

Cordial in a crowd but known to thrive alone. Solitude. Strength. Complexity. It is why I love wolves. They flourish as grey shade characters among animals. They care, but pounce. Alert. Always. Maybe I love wolves because I am one. Always running, but stopping to care. Attacking, but healing the wounded. A paradoxical nightmare. So complicated, I don't understand myself sometimes. Wanting to be alone but needing my pack. A lone wolf knows its strength, when it howls, it sends chills down everyone's spines. Yet, when it calls, it calls for its pack. Wolves and I, we can live alone, but are always stronger alongside our own—no matter how complex we are. They remind me of my dual strength: fraternity and togetherness, seclusion and retirement. It is why I love wolves.

Rhythm And Blues

It's more than just music. It's the rhythm of our souls, together. It's the way you walk and talk and dress and breathe. The Bluetooth speakers are loud. Loud enough to feel the beat in your body, traveling from your head to your shoulders to your ribs to your legs to your toes. It's everywhere. Let it consume you.

It's more than just music. You feel the dancers tease you, the words rolling off your tongue because it's all orchestrated. Verse, chorus, verse, chorus again and again until it's not just stuck in your head but the rhythm and your heartbeat becomes one.

It's more than just music. It's a state of mind, a constant reminder, a ringing alarm.

Avarice

Eternity is only the universe, the soul, and the avarice of mundanes.

Scenery

The space between these two arms,
Holds a body of regret and contradictions.
Hollow opinions surface from
Seas of ambiguity and doubt.
Five feet and a few inches above the ground,
stands taut muscle and aspiring thigh gaps.
A city of apologies forms in the chest cavity,
Gardens of reminiscence bloom
Beside the erratically pumping heart.
Sharp thorns of thought embed into skin,
While the plague takes over the brain.
The bend of the elbow of holds secrets,
Uttered by the voice behind the shell of the ear.

To Be A Poet

Weave your woes such that the cries escaping your lips sound like astounding music to others. That is what it is to be a poet.

Red Ink Street

You asked me why I never wrote
Why I never told.
But I wasn't silent!
That quill wrote only in blood,
From my body that only lived for you
I wrote till my heart gave up
But you were too blind in her eyes to see,
Me; I was gasping for help
On the sidewalk from across your street

Fuel

I think it's tragic how passion dims into monotony.

Eventually, all that ever was and all there ever will be will fade into oblivion.

So, wake up. Give more than the seven billion half-alive people on this planet.

Go be reckless one more time.

Who We Were, Who We Are

Chipped porcelain cups that you keep deep inside your cabinet clatter forward, smashing onto the ground and you're pulled back into a memory of grey skies and rain weaving with the tears on your face, the mud clinging to your knees as you drop down and the rapid beat of your heart, that seemed never-ending.

You can't forget, can you? You've lived a pretence for the past seven years.

How long will it take? You asked that day on the doorstep seven years ago as you cleared your house out and fled because every breath inhaled there felt virulent. Left the place you called home because the emptiness was unbearable because home isn't cement and bricks, it's a person. And that home crumbled into ashes long back.

Seven years it took you to completely bury that part of yourself inside, to fill the hole left behind with half kept promises and silences of the past.

Seven years; since you threw away that cup of earl grey tea, stale and cold in the porcelain cup; the aroma still nauseates you.

Seven years later, you stand above the broken shards of porcelain, the last reminder of the one you lost bringing all of it surging back, like water decimating the walls of the dam with all the force it can convoke and destroying everything around.

Time doesn't heal all wounds; some nestle in the corners of lost memories and some only deepen with it. Time itself is a wound, a reminder of everything lost.

Maybe seven years isn't enough;

Maybe forever won't be either.

Haemorrhage

The clouds were bleeding. They were cut open by heavy sparks of lightning and all I could imagine was rain in the colour of thick rich blood pouring from their flesh. The sky was the colour of the newspaper strewn on the porch this morning; a dull grey with birds imitating black specks of ink. It was hard to think about anything; my head felt like a block of wood, uncut and rough.

The Fragments of a Memory

It's rather selfish. Selfish to hold on to a memory, a fragment of the past which I should have buried a long time ago as I had promised myself. Yet here I am, using nostalgia as an excuse to think about it to make myself feel the way I did when it happened. Good. You would think the impact of it dwindles with time because with time, memories fade, and things that mattered most don't anymore. But unlike the others, it never does with you. Maybe someday I will finally move on, but today I blame nostalgia as an excuse to revisit the memory of you.

Calling Constellation

I'm going far away
To live within the stars
Tell mother not to wait
For tonight I won't dine

I'm going far away
Where the evil can't find me
Humans are the vilest creatures
Tell brother this is not a game of hide and seek

I shall live in the universe
Among superior celestial bodies
I shall knock on each doorstep to say sorry;
I'm about to leave, but before I go

Will you tell my friend and my lover?
My mother and my brother
I love them, they are my world
But it's time I found my place in this universe.

Can these stars absorb me?
So that I become just one of the things that make them shine
Am I at least pure for the universe;
Not free of sin, but not full of it
That I become another calling constellation?

Twin Flames

It shouldn't be so easy to fit in your arms,
To pull you closer.
It simply can't be so simple,
The way our fingers intertwine.

I refuse to believe that I could fall
For someone like you, yet again.
But it seems so effortless as if
somehow my every curve
Was shaped for you.

The way we were *made to love* is simply not in our control.

Connotation

We bleed words of despair onto the parchment,
Trying to fit every emotion coursing through our veins into poetry.

Strange, how we bedeck our pain.

Fortissimo

One day these whites and blacks
Will forgo everything I lack.
My hands will stretch
To the notes I wish
Were under my control;

My wrists will drop and roll
Swoop and trill
Creating laces and frills
For pieces I perfect
Maybe then I will respect
All I have to offer,
So, it won't bother
Me anymore
How I couldn't earlier

But I will
Remember the failure.

Mortality

Our lives are too short to gratify our hubris;

to be viewed with eyes of pathos- we are strung to it with the uncertainty of morality.

What is today shall not be tomorrow for tomorrow is not promised. You haven't seen it, nor have I; for all, we know it may not exist for one of us or both.

Will you succumb to the downfalls of humanity and let ruthlessness and insecurity hinder you to love and be loved?

Valiant

We had sat silent long enough
Weights tied to our legs
Oppression weighed too much,
And patriarchy broke the scale.
How can one rise from such bondage?
Rise like we have?
It took will power and determination,
I tell my grandchildren
We fought till 'a little more' equality
Helped each other,
All around the world, we are united
And that's how.

We broke the shackles, the weights and the glass ceiling above us;
But there's still a long way to go.
Remain valiant,
I will tell my grandchildren
Be a good man, be a valiant woman,
For this is a long fight,
I will tell my grandchildren.

Reverie

One day, we'll tell our kids
How we were the fairy princesses and princes
They read about, in their fairy tales.

We'll tell them
About the times we stumbled
Upon ponds and toadstools,

And how
We spent our summers in the forest,
Climbing trees and foraging for fairy rings.

There were times if you were quiet enough,
Within the shadows of the garden,
You could hear the elves frolicking.

But many say fairytales aren't real,
And that forest folk don't exist,
But they haven't ventured past anything yet.

Mithridatism

The world seems to spin around and stop altogether at the same time.

Only when you understand true pain is when you become unassailable.

Words echo through my head as I try to anchor myself, trying to get a hold of anything to stop the anguish in the pit of my stomach.

Be vulnerable to nothing, poison is only a start.

I think as a flood of nausea takes over and sends me toppling to the ground.

Every time you do this, you're one step closer to ascendancy.

'Why do this?' my subconscious asks. There's no choice. If I stop, I will lose all the work of sleepless nights filled with paranoia. All those nights spent enduring pain will fade in vain. But as my throat feels assaulted by a thousand knives and muscles clench painfully, letting go doesn't seem incongruous.

Poison won't kill you if you kill it first.

My vision seems to waver, and my limbs feel numb as it courses through my body and the poison induced stupor slowly kicks in.

There is no escape, you can't stop this, you chose this.

I think as I glance at the vials of poison kept on the bureau.

Only your whole life, then you can finally sleep after.

The last thing I hear is the clatter of glass on the ground, the first of many vials I drink that night.

Who said that power came without a price?

Girdling

From the pines on the mountains of my hand
To the prairies and wildflowers
on the plains of my thighs,
Birds migrate.

(I welcome their arrival with grandiosity)

They peck at the woods of my skin
Making themselves home
When they leave,
Wispy white feathers fall on my body
Reminding me that their return is
Assured.

Outlook

Why must we call those who have the resilience to go on after enduring the horrors of this wicked world *'victims'* neglecting what they truly are - *survivors*.

It's time we rethink our outlook on how things truly are.

Combat, Punch

My mouth bleeds profusely, but today, I refuse ointment. I refuse to lose another match. I punched back, hoping it was hard enough. It falls to the ground. I see shock on its face. Wait, how did I do that? It throws a predictable punch. Punch blocked. This is crazy. I know its next move, it goes for my face, but I attack it right in the head. That's what it gets for living in mine. How am I doing this? Why is it not getting up? Is it…dead? I turn around in relief, but it grabs me by the neck. Time to fight again. I look at the scoreboard- it says, "Healing."

Deception

They say eyes are the windows to the soul, but yours were ebony-like obsidians.

Dead roses dripping from your lips and your voice was like rich velvet, fabricating each and every word,

"I promise I won't leave."

Remind me to turn your empty words into a book.

Recherché

She was an ocean of raging water,
like biting winter,
bleakness percolating through every touch.
But they chose burning fire,
the crackle of ferocity and the heat of new spring,
over the frigidity of her caress and the placidity of her presence,
Because at the end of the day

Fire still burns sharper than the sting of ice.

Default Network Mode

Maybe it is this comfortable because we know what to say when. Not in a way that is calculated, but the air around us is liberating to say the least. Every word seems to have its place; silence nestles snuggly between the pauses of our sentences. It is tranquil and white and pastel. I see conversations in colours. I see them in pictures. We may be painting in half-silence right now but in my head we're on a beach watching the sun set. I am daydreaming in a daydream. That's how it is with you.

Yearning

I crave you like a man does an oasis in a desert,
with sheer desperation and a pinch of hope.

Silly Girl

No one's coming to save you
Silly girl,
Learn to live on your own
Fend for yourself
Every man for himself.

No one's coming to help you
Silly girl,
This is a man's place; it is his world.
The lady, the outcast, people who love differently,
Nothing was ever built for them!
No one's coming to support you

Silly girl,
You are strong enough on your own
Go save the world
Even those unkind to you

If you can forgive,
You are tenacious enough.

Silly girl,

They need you now
The time has come
You are not so silly anymore.

Monochromatic

The memories I have of us are black and white, leached colourless by the moon.

Azoth

Do you remember when we were kids? Plucking out flowers from small bushes and throwing grass at each other's hair, bursting into fits of laughter.

Do you remember learning to ride a bicycle; falling on the coarse ground and comparing scars? Or when we cycled in the rain, speeding through the boulevard and speckling water from the puddles and sitting in the wet grass after. Things were easy, peaceful. Actions lacked caution; It didn't feel like we were walking on broken glass.

Do you remember when we ate food like it was the last time, carefree and heedless? Now it feels far away; now we're self-conscious and deliberate. Now, we spend hours in front of the mirror, scowling at the unfamiliar reflection that stares back. Looking for a long-lost glimpse of familiarity.

Do you remember when the biggest worries were running fast enough to win that last slice of cake? Now we're running away from everything; the reckless adrenaline washed out by overwhelming stress.

Let's go back to careless days when our hands were too small to hold jars of cookies and legs just a tad too short to keep running.

Let's go back to watching the frail petals of dandelions flow away with the breeze in comfortable silence, amnesic and unfamiliar with the world out there.

End Line

Echoey cries
Skids and skid marks
Rhythmic thumps and
Sweaty sparks

Calculated steps
Closely coordinated
Endless practices
(Quite the overstatement)

Drenched in sweat and dirt
Chests falling and rising
Cheers from the side-lines:
Energizing.

Breathless 'Well-Played's
Honorific pats
Sorry for that foul
I shouldn't have, my bad

A tapped hand,
Unexpected halts
A forced slip
It wasn't even my fault

Cautious defence
Hands forever raised
Charging offense
I promise, it was just a mistake.

Left, right, convert.
Fall for the rebound
Push yourself, push the team
This is your battleground.

To my 'friend'

There are so many things I wish to tell you still;

But there are even more questions that I wish to ask.

How does freedom feel? To be your person, not confined to anyone else's point of view. Not having to live up to anyone's expectations because you are your person? Liberating? You're allowed to find solace in my absence, I've only ever wanted you to be happy. You know that, right?

You're allowed to find new friends, new passions, you're allowed to discover more about yourself and undertake every adventure which once frightened you. You are allowed to move on.

As am I.

I pushed away everyone else because I thought I will always have you and that was enough to replace the world.

Often what feels perpetual isn't always there and what you were most tentative for is the only thing tenacious.

And that is okay.

Acknowledgements

Harshita

Thank you, mother, for always believing in my potential and supporting me in every decision, one of which is 'Meraki'. You are always in my heart and without you, I am lost. Amamma and Tatha, thank you for your love and affectionate embrace that I always keep with me. Anshdeep Singh Bhachoo, Shikha Singh Bhachoo and Amandeep Singh Bhachoo, thank you for being my second home, I am forever grateful for your kindness. And to my dearest friends, who have always cheered on my triumphs and stood by me during my failures. To my favourite artist, NF, who probably isn't reading this, but whose songs remain my constant inspiration; 'Nate' literally raised me. And of course, my co-authors. I am indebted to you all for joining my website, and for what has blossomed into a lasting friendship, of which Meraki remains a symbol, it only immortalises the mark we made in this world. Lastly, to Harshita. I hope you look back here whenever you feel low, I hope you can call this book "home".

Alisha

I don't think 'Meraki' would have been possible without the unwavering support from my family and friends. Mom and Dad, thank you for always believing in me and bringing me back to Earth when my head was too far up the clouds. My grandparents also played a crucial role, in being with me from the start. Their kindness and love are something I deeply cherish. I'm so grateful for Aaliya, Saanvi and Niven for not only being my anchor but my muse, and at times, even my second home. Jehaan also wanted a special mention, hi Jehaan *waves*.

Last but foremost, 'Meraki' was a journey of about 6-7 months with probably the most amazing group of writers. The four of you constantly leave me in awe. From exchanging Spotify usernames to writing a whole book together, I couldn't be more grateful.

Adwita

'Meraki' has been a roller coaster of a journey and I'm thankful for each moment that led up to it. I would like to thank my parents for their constant support and encouragement to try new things and nurturing my interests to the best of their ability. To my sister, whom I hope to make an impression on through this small piece of myself that is Meraki. To Taylor Swift and a never-ending playlist of classical music, a constant abode of comfort. I'd also like to extend my gratitude to Wolfishwordss, a cogent milestone without which I wouldn't have come this far as a writer. I'm undoubtedly grateful to my friends for all their support. To all the books I've read; the crisp pages that kept me up, thinking. And of course, no acknowledgement is complete without thanking my co-authors, for getting me out of writing slumps and without whom this chaotic venture would not have been possible. At last, I'd like to thank my past self, for being the epitome of annoying optimism and hope, who chose to get up and keep going. Thank you, and I hope 'Meraki' was as much of an enthralling experience for you, as it was for me.

Acknowledgements

Divita

I would like to thank my co-authors for this experience and for walking the journey alongside me. It has been absolutely wonderful knowing these four people whose varied outlook on life never fails to teach me. Without Harshita's spark of an idea, I wouldn't have even thought of getting myself published. I would also extend gratitude towards my middle school English teacher, Sumithra Krishnan, who always pushed me to recite my barely decent poetry and prose to her. I wouldn't have been continually interested in improving if it wasn't for her. My family, of course, plays a huge role in nurturing my interests and meeting my needs and I am always grateful for their contribution. To my friends- I feel at peace knowing I have your support. My acknowledgement would be incomplete without the mention of my favourite artist, the ever-inspiring BTS, who I hold uncomfortably close to my heart and whose songs have been played throughout the writing process of 'Meraki'. And to all the books read. Thank you.

Shreya

I would like to acknowledge my internet friends, for looking forward to this with so much zeal.

The authors and poets I look up to and my co-authors for accompanying me in What is most definitely one of the greatest achievements in my life so far. My grandparents- Nana-Nani and Dada-Dadi.

Lastly, I would like to extend my gratitude toward Lana Del Rey, your music inspires me. You made Meraki possible. Thank you.

Meet the Co-Authors

Harshita Ray

Harshita is a passionate writer who has been writing since she was nine. She may not write very often, but only when inspiration strikes. She believes that this helps her bring out raw emotions rather than throwing in a piece just for the sake of it. Every piece in Meraki was woven intricately in her mind and put onto paper, and she hopes you enjoy the embroidered result. Her hobbies apart from writing include playing Basketball. Find Harshita on Instagram: @raysverses.

Harshita manages a website for writers, of writers and by writers, Wolfishwordss, on Instagram: @wolfishwordss, link: wolfishwordss.wordpress.com

Alisha Rai

Alisha is a spirited feminist, environmentalist and an animal lover, who admires of all kinds of art. She is a nostalgic writer and never misses a chance to record videos or take pictures, keeping her camera handy. She enjoys travelling, and has been a nomad from childhood, shifting homes from a young age. Playing basketball and painting are amongst her favourite hobbies.

Find her on Instagram: @alishaaa.rai

Adwita Agrahari

Adwita is an articulate writer whose pieces, introspective in nature, explore themes of realistic escapism and she looks for inspiration in the most common fragments of life. As a voracious reader, she admires different forms of art and self-expression, with a benign spot for ballet and literature. She also enjoys classical music and spends a lot of time playing the keyboard.

Find her on Instagram: @adwita.a

Divita Joshi

Writing to Divita is the equivalent of a log in a diary or journal, containing some pieces more sophisticated than others. Aside from writing, she also takes an ardent interest in music, reading, and playing the piano. She loves playing football and basketball.

Find her on Instagram: @wherejoonwhere

Shreya Banerji

Shreya is an ambitious writer whose resourcefulness is evident in twelve of her pieces published in this anthology. On an average day, you will find her religiously curled up to read her classic favourites or watching MasterChef clips on YouTube with her spitz Arlo. A writer in various blogs and websites, it brings her utmost joy to be a published author. A strong believer in the power of real-life experience, she loves to engage with art that tells stories, art that displays raw emotions. Be it the music she enjoys or the books she reads, she is always listening.

Find her on Instagram: @shreyabanerjii_

INKFEATHERS PUBLISHING

India's Most Author Friendly Publishing House

Stay updated about the latest books, anthologies, events, exclusive offers, contests, product giveaways and other things that we do to support authors.

 Inkfeathers Publishing

 @InkfeathersPublishing

@_Inkfeathers

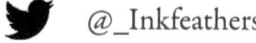 @Inkfeathers

 Inkfeathers.com

We'd love to connect with you!

www.ingramcontent.com/pod-product-compliance
Ingram Content Group UK Ltd.
Pitfield, Milton Keynes, MK11 3LW, UK
UKHW042118230426
12064UKWH00003B/210